FIRSTMATTERPRESS
Portland, Ore.

THE GROWTH LINES

THE GROWTH LINES

gabby hancher

FIRSTMATTERPRESS
Portland, Ore.

Copyright © 2021 by Gabby Hancher
All rights reserved

First Edition

Published in the United States
by First Matter Press
Portland, Oregon

Paperback ISBN 978-1-7338246-7-5

Edited by Lauren Paredes, Andra Vltavín,
Caroline Wilcox Reul & Ash Good

Cover Illustration
Copyright © 2021 by Aleksandra Apocalisse
apocalisseart.com

Book design by Ash Good
ashgood.com

FIRSTMATTERPRESS.ORG

To my grandma, Diana,
who taught me the power of magic and nature.
Hope the fifth dimension is as exciting
as you'd hoped, Grams.

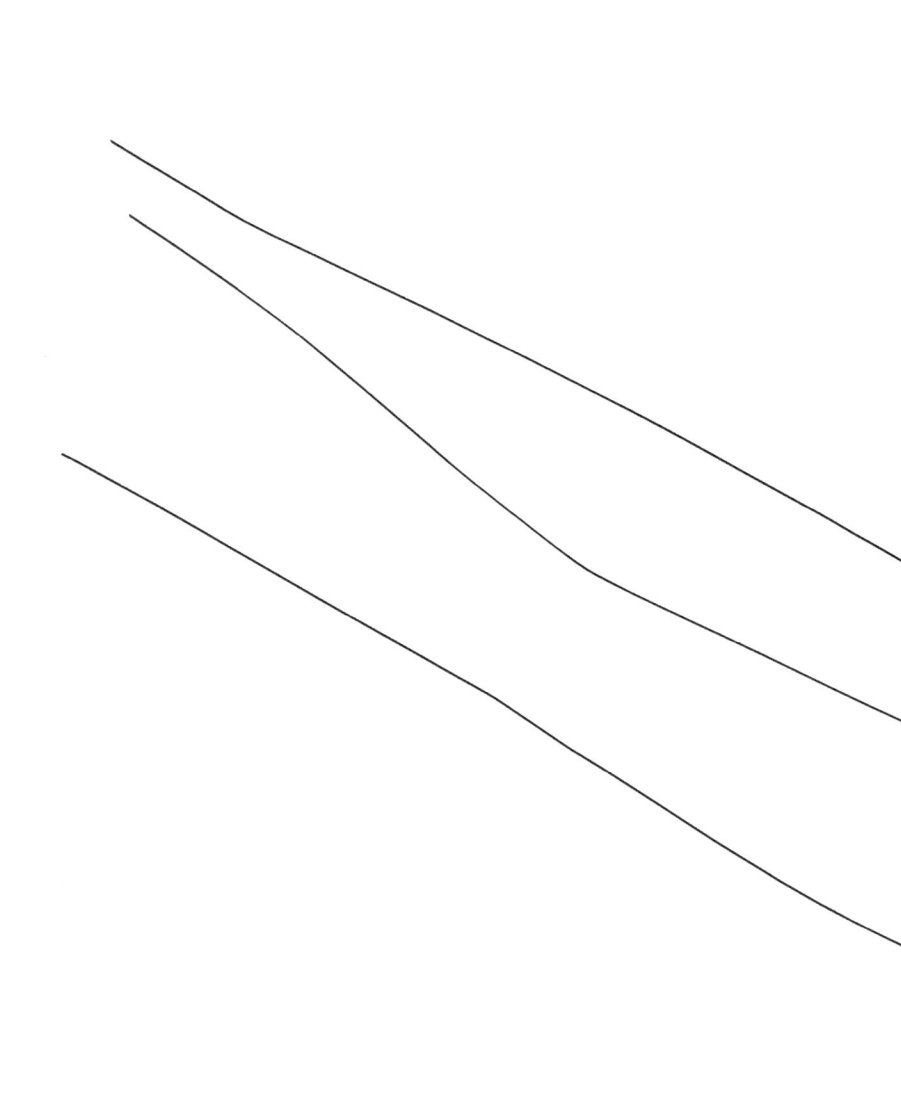

"it is a serious thing

*just to be alive
on this fresh morning
in the broken world"*

—MARY OLIVER, *INVITATION*

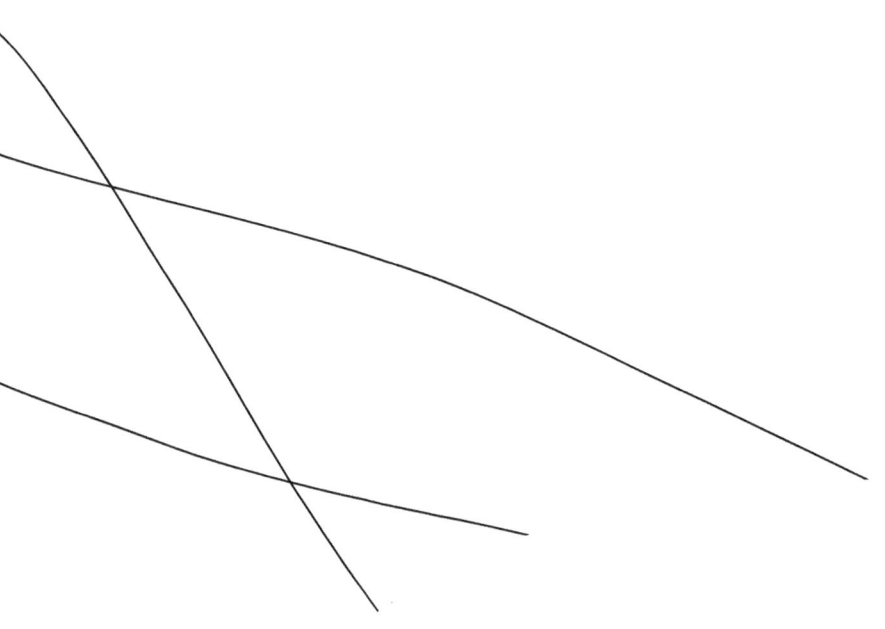

birth rite

- 7   sound, a maiden voyage
- 8   on the business of being born
- 13   the alchemist
- 15   let me show you how to love me
- 17   when you are a body
- 18   a mother does create

grief portal

- 23   let's talk transformation
- 24   you are narcissus but i am not your reflection
- 25   inheritance
- 27   i was made to burn this landscape to the ground
- 28   avoidance
- 30   resilience

awakening

35 you slip out of a wet chrysalis
36 breathing
38 queer roots
40 an offering to my inner world
41 the temple of our soft bellies
42 a circle turns in on itself

45 acknowledgments

BIRTH RITE

*sound, a maiden voyage
every tremor & change in pitch
asking me to wake up
to the great & terrible beauty
of being in a body*

on the business of being born

i'm in darkness
it's my first time in this place
or else i've been here before
i think maybe i'm arriving
but when i ask, the universe sighs
& starts braiding chlorophyll into my hair

i would say it's a lot like the womb
but i've never been there
or else i have, but the memory leaves a hole
where my mind will someday form
& i'm left wondering
if my mother really did stop dinner for my arrival

it's possible i'm screaming
but the sound is muffled by dirt or else i have no mouth
& the business of being born is a strange one
i could tell you about all the pieces of me
but they will someday become something else
made of the same recycled stardust

despite this orchestrated chaos
my roots grow down into legs,
& the universe begins to hum
my true name over & over & over
so i can feel my way through the entanglement
until i'm certain that there's nothing left to do but grow
toward what i will soon remember is the sun

blooming isn't easy,
& it's good to remember
a lot of people
have done it
before me

the alchemist

she told me there was light vibrating
down my spine — through the body

so i practice this strange alchemy
hearing the way light transforms
to darkness & back to light

dual serpents coil tighter
toward each other, their curling
scales scaffolding my being

lips part & melodic tributaries erupt outward

snakes are actually unborn sentences
i am overflowing with them
then our hands meet in holy palmers' kiss —

i cannot contain what joy feels like
in my own skin so i'm giving it to you

you receive my creation as if you had always known
the sound of being alive

let me show you how to love me

untangle cosmic weeds for true vision
nature made to fall deeply
to be taught in so many ways
what *unconditional* looks like,
tastes like, smells like

i am ready to be seen
shed hallowed armor
that my hands can remember
how i like to be touched
in present tense
just like that, yes like that

& god when this incubation is done
my heart, your heart,
circling & encircled
differentiated dances
of nourishment

& what else is there but to be loved so wholly?

when you are a body

ripe for the earth
nesting soft in lichen & moss
remember the dream i had for us

where you are soil again
home to fungus & forest spirits.
remember, too, the complexity of love

when you are decay, a mycelium network
searching for home among my roots

remember how i held you, pink & trembling

a mother does create

turn up the heat, find the steady rhythm of the pelvis
connected by a thread to many other bodies
punctuated by rich astrological history

pour in salt, the entire bag
float belly up in domestic ocean, birthing permissions:
self-portrait reflected on hungry thighs, glistening
                                                        ritual in the dark

whispers in the rise & fall of a tide-reflected moon
mother's hands to belly, warm & inviting
oh, what will we make here today?

fingertips to lips shaking stories into existence
a sacred tremble between smoke & water
let it all rest there, pregnant pause

the threshold is open

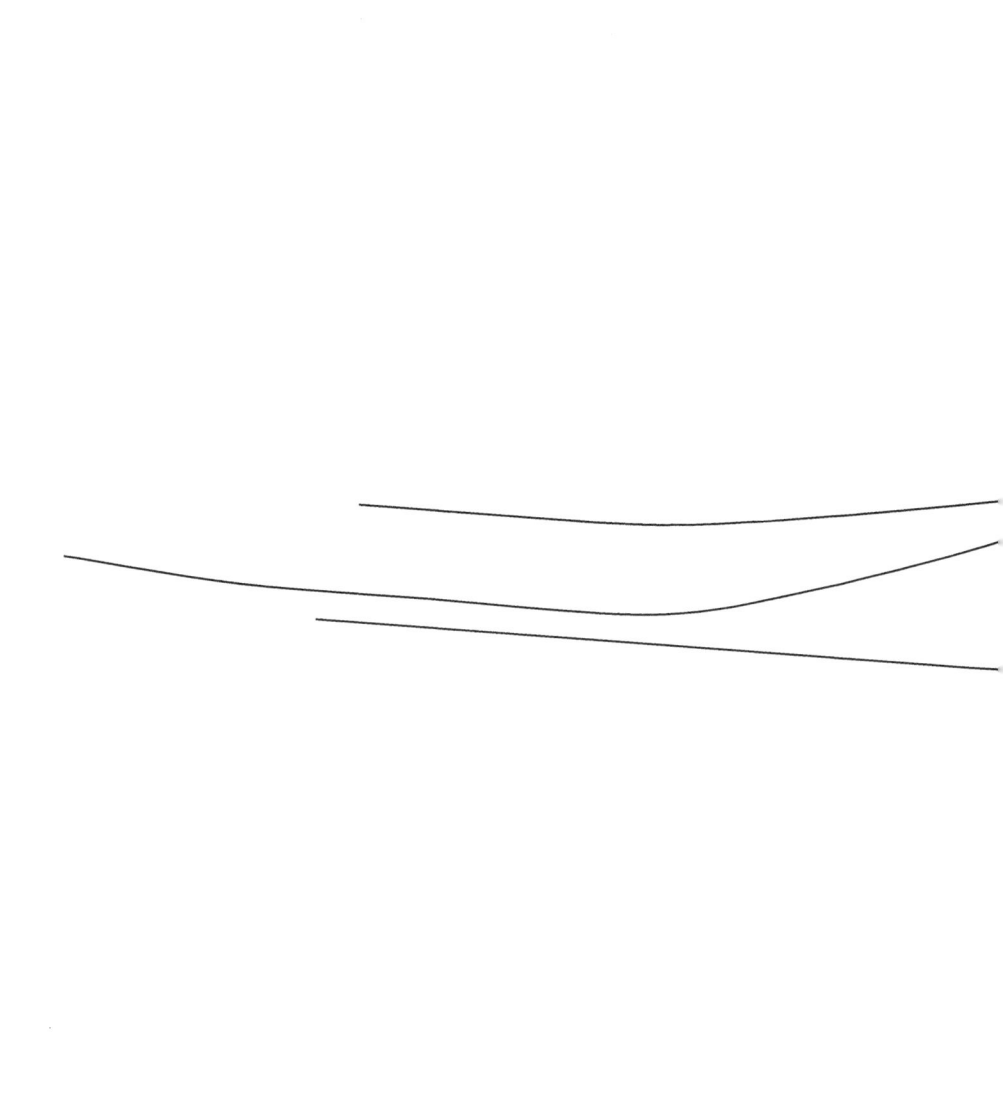

GRIEF PORTAL

let's talk transformation.
twin snakes whisper how will you unearth yourself?

boundaries shift like tectonic plates between us
an egress opens, & we leave old skins behind

you are narcissus but i am not your reflection

or i am but to survive
your sweet mirrored nymph
a watery vision of codependency

i want to crack you open wide
reveal the warped, silvery foundation
so you can see the mess we've made

inheritance

this season i watch my mind
worn neural pathways that spiral outward
until the networks gleam like city lights

then zoom in to the head of a needle
as burning brilliance becomes blinding heartache
indistinguishable from the way everything must die

shame slides into the corners
of my eyes until i'm seeing
the shape of her in the dark again

wondering if this is my inheritance

the child self hasn't learned words yet
tears every single book from the shelf
searching for a reminder of how badly
i wanted to befriend stinging bees in spring
how stars are dead but still light our paths
that this is all just a story passed down by old hands

i was made to burn this landscape to the ground

not in my lifetime
you say, praying nightly
but i was not made in your image
property was never holier than people
your silence hangs heavy on the pulpit
what is left except to unleash the fury of generations past
upon all your diligently hoarded finery
reject your offer of easily afforded comfort
disrobe mine again & again
howling grief into the night
hymns for the fall of capitalism
set injustice ablaze

avoidance

throat clenches
tight discord
inflammation

      anxiety croons
      what a bullshit performance
      eat away at ego
      sickening crunch
      you are bathed in red

            it's hard to be alone
            it's hard to be alone
            like this
            breathing catches fire

shake the body
overwhelm overwhelm
lion breath
shake again to be sure

        it's hard to be alone
        it's hard to be alone
        cooling breath

                open mouth sigh
                animal releases
                i watch & say
                thank you

resilience

feet perched at the edge
centuries of the erosion cycle underneath
no vision beyond
ghostly curls of human smoke

the void renders dancing moonlight
cast across celestial bodies
while ancestors sing their well-kept secrets
i am so cosmically small

the fear tastes bitter & metallic
earth agrees, helps me
vomit up decades of unsaid things

suddenly lighter than ever,
i leap into the great wave of nothing
on the other side is hope

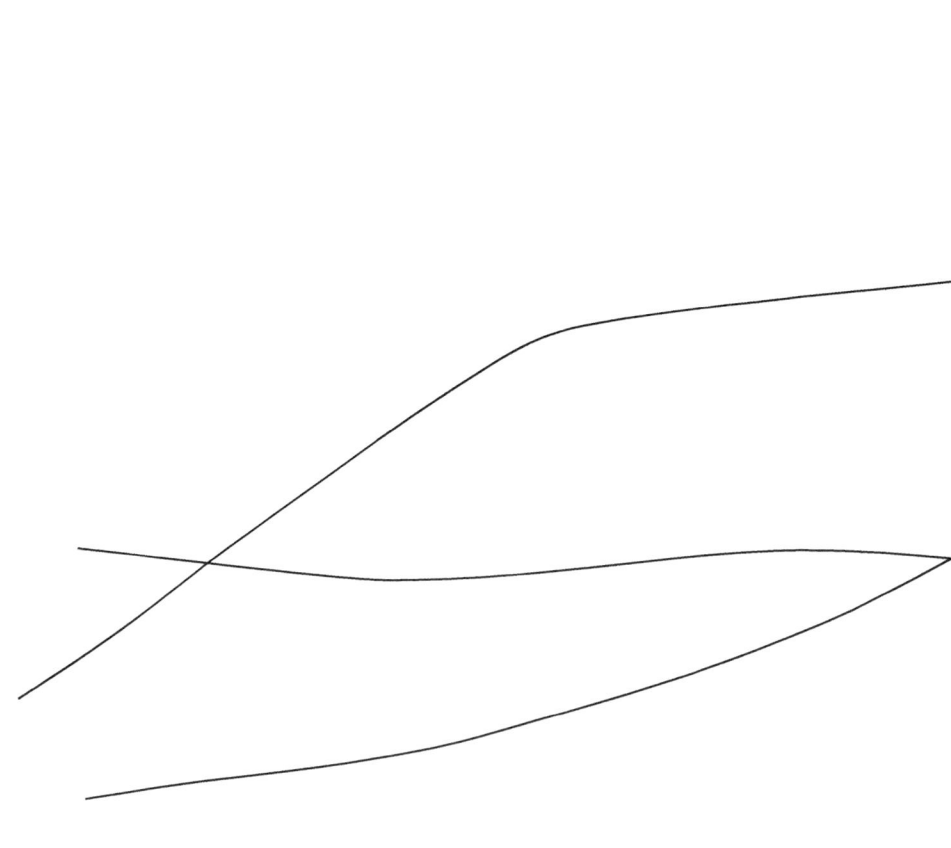

AWAKE
NING

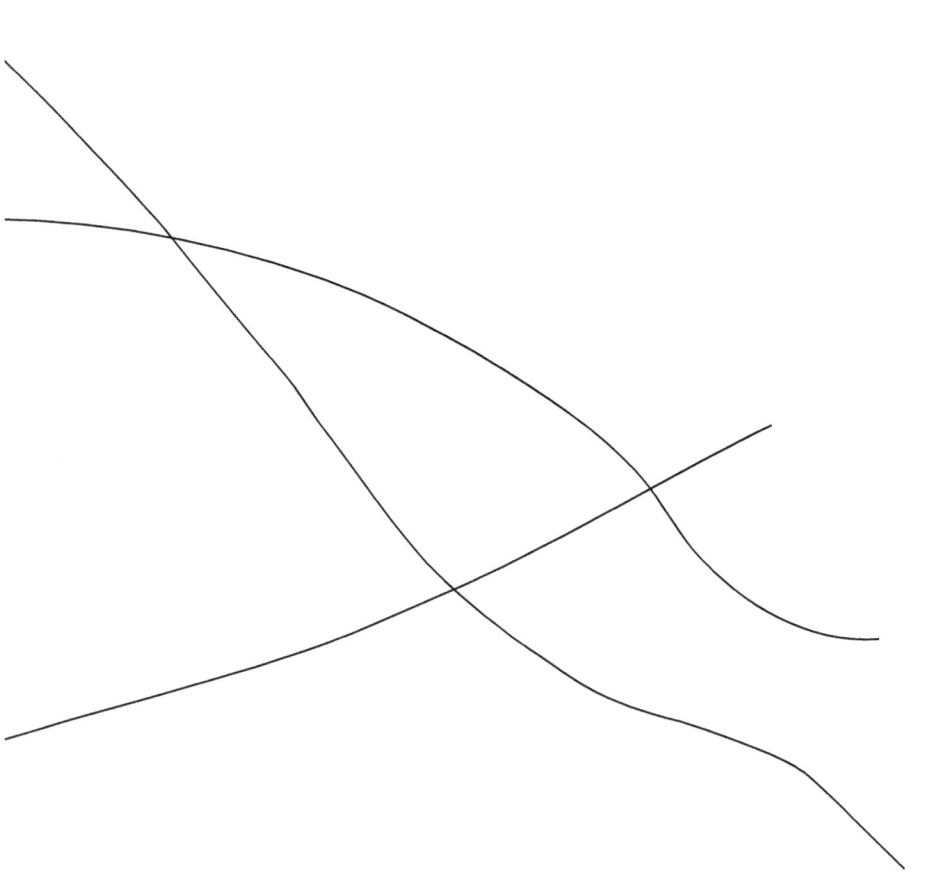

you slip out of a wet chrysalis, sweet & warm
into love, out of love & back again
darling, please forgive yourself for growing
& let the soft animal of your body love what it loves
until your own pleasures are again
the birth of you

* *collage poem, see page 45 for acknowledgments*

breathing

left lobe inflates

for the first time not dissecting
every period that comes at the end
of an unfamiliar dialogue
but bearing witness
to migrating thoughts
searching for their destination

careen into routine ungracefully
inhale, exhale,
forward fold, forward fall
toward chaotic beauty
more spaciousness
than what was remembered

right lobe inflates

today: presence

queer roots

i hadn't known you yet
sweet seeds were planted
but denied essential nourishment
a growth cycle spent
watering sapphic enmeshment

yet here i am
welcoming you into my life
i won't hide this galaxy brain body anymore —
witness my blooming, my unfolding
my becoming

fertilize this transformation,
until the tender blooms unfurl
out of this soft earth
let it be perfectly messy —
a reflection of all possibilities
in this lifetime

& when i kiss my beautiful husband each night
marveling at our holographic existence
tasting the sweetness of it on my tongue
i know my queer roots run deep

an offering to my inner world

i found her in my dusty chalk fingers
sun-burnt nose, cheeky grin
arranging my worries into bouquets
sense-making in all that darkness

we stop on our walk to smell every bloom
name every four-legged friend we happen upon
then settle for art making on the concrete
tell me again, what is the color of thriving?

the temple of our soft bellies

earth vessel
feasting on joy & delight

reclaim her with rest
extend wide into her shifting spaciousness

count breath instead of calories
study the growth lines on her thighs as sacred text

body hair & all
cosmically asymmetrical

offer devotion to her sloping altars of bone & sinew
until they are known by their true name

yours

a circle turns in on itself

becomes something else
is transformed in the witnessing

& when i witness you,
i am there to gather you, like a woman in the woods
who delicately places each fine berry in her basket

each turn of the wheel is a cardinal reminder
to offer you my hands for holding
to accept you as you are

in circle, i am reminded of this

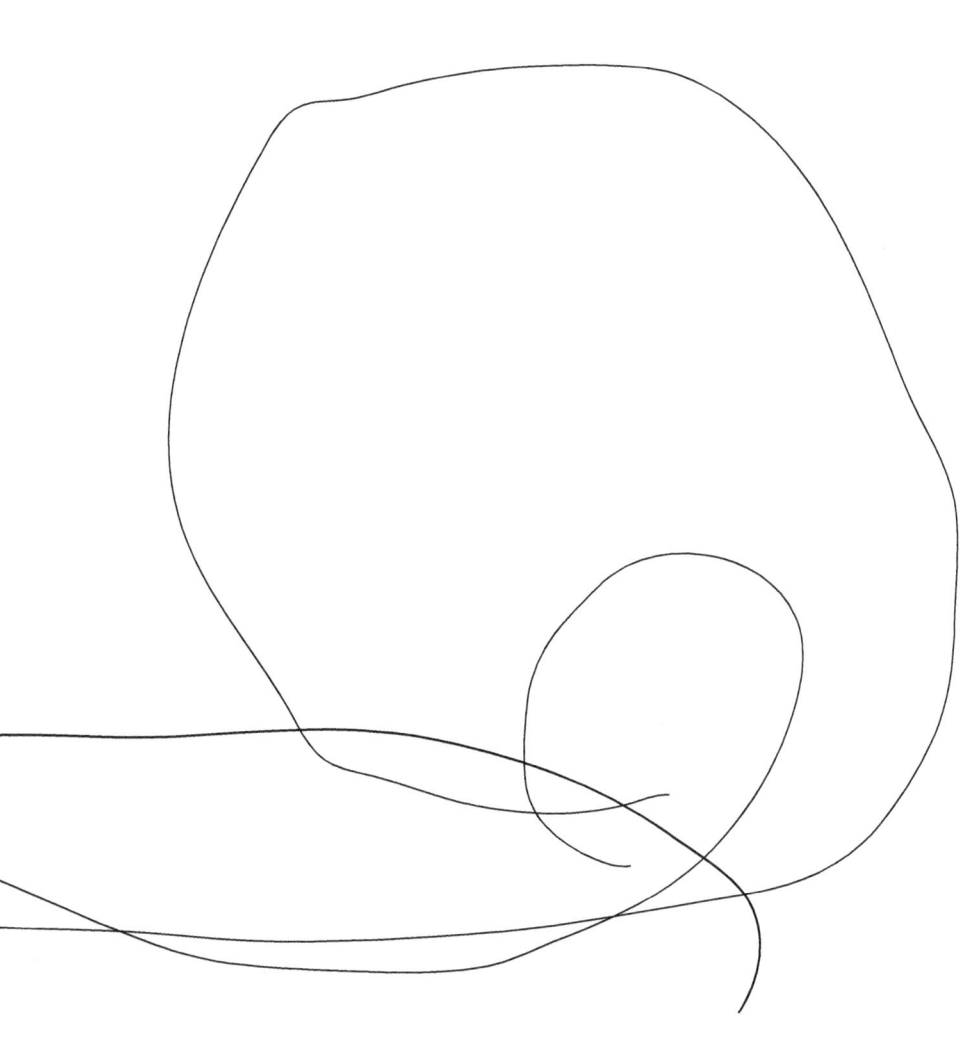

ACKNOWLEDGMENTS

The poem that appears on page 35 is a collage of lines by Julia Bray ("you slip out of a wet chrysalis, sweet & warm"), Lunita Valeria Velásquez ("into love, out of love & back again"), Ash Good ("forgive yourself for growing"), Mary Oliver ("let the soft animal of your body love what it loves") & Andra Light ("until your own pleasures are again the birth of you"). It was inspired by the 4 New Moons poetry reading on April 22, 2020.

Versions of these poems have appeared in the following publications:

Salmon Creek Journal: "queer roots"

High Priestesses of Poetry: An Anthology, Volume 1: "on the business of being born," "the alchemist"

High Priestess of Poetry: An Anthology, Volume 2: "a mother does create," "inheritance"

GABBY HANCHER (she/they) is a queer creator and magic maker from Portland, Oregon. As a writer, she mindfully explores the intersection between trauma and resilience, calling upon nature and childhood for illumination. The alchemy of art and science is the crux of Gabby's playful light, seeking to help others unite mind, body and spirit in accessible, compassionate ways. They are currently a counselor-in-training with a special interest in the Hakomi method and attachment work. Outside of writing, Gabby can be found dancing, enjoying nature and studying embodied social justice practices.

PORTRAIT **STEVEN HANCHER**

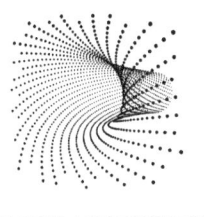

FIRSTMATTERPRESS
Portland, Ore.

SELECTED TITLES FROM FIRST MATTER PRESS

BODY UNTIL LIGHT
K.M. Lighthouse

CONSIDER THE BODY, WINGED
Jessica E. Pierce

IT'S JUST YOU & ME, MISS MOON
Emily Moon

LOVERS AND OTHER STILL CREATURES
Eitan Codish

OTHERWISE, MAGIC
Lauren Paredes

ROUTES BETWEEN RAINDROPS
Dan Wiencek

THE GROWTH LINES
Gabby Hancher

THE NIGHT SKY IS A PLACE WHERE THINGS GET LOST
Andrew Chenevert

WE ARE NOT READY FOR WHAT WE ARE
Ash Good

FIRSTMATTERPRESS.ORG

www.ingramcontent.com/pod-product-compliance
Lightning Source LLC
Chambersburg PA
CBHW061212070526
44583CB00025B/3218